LEARN OPPOSITES

with the

MUNCH BUNCH

© 1981 Rourke Publications, Inc.
© 1981 Studio Publications, Ltd.

Library of Congress in Publication Data

Reed, Giles.
  Learn opposites with the Munch Bunch.

  Summary: The members of the Munch Bunch
enjoy various activities which illustrate
pairs of words with opposite meanings.
    1. English language—Synonyms and antonyms—
Juvenile literature. 1. Mitson, Angela, ill.
II. Title.
PE1591.R43   1981   428.1   81-11986
ISBN 0-86625-078-6   AACR2

Rourke Publications, Inc.
Windermere, FL   32786

FAST   **Runner Bean runs** fast

SLOW   **Tom Tomato runs** slowly

TALL   Suzie Celery is tall

SHORT Olive is short

HAPPY   **Scruff Gooseberry is** happy

SAD   **Olly Onion is** sad

EMPTY   Pippa Pear's jar is empty

FULL   Emma Apple's jar is full

THICK Tom Tomato is using thick wood

THIN Bounce is using thin wood

LIGHT   Adam Avocado's parcel is light

HEAVY   Casper Carrot's parcel is heavy

PUSH Zack Zucchini and Supercool are pushing the car

PULL Corky Coconut is pulling the car

STRAIGHT Sally has painted straight lines

CROOKED Pete has painted crooked lines

HOT   Pedro Orange is thinking of the hot sunshine

COLD   Lucy and Pedro are in the cold snow

OPEN

CLOSED

Casper Carrot's door is open

Spud's door is closed

DRY   Billy and Scruff are dry

WET   Emma Apple is wet

CLEAN   Most of Lizzie Leek's washing is clean

DIRTY   One of Lizzie's sheets is dirty

UP   Bounce is up in the air

DOWN Pippa Pear is down on the ground

FRONT   In the mirror we can see the front of Emma Apple

BACK   We can see the back of Emma

SHOUT   **Wally Walnut is** shouting

WHISPER   **Penny Parsnip is** whispering

ON   Water is coming out of the faucet
which is on
OFF The other faucet is turned off

NARROW The frame is narrow where Scruff
is playing
WIDE The frame is wide where Billy is sitting

LITTLE Olive has got a little ice cream

LARGE Supercool has got a large ice cream

ASLEEP   **Slippy Banana is** asleep

AWAKE   **Skid and Barney are** awake

START Button Mushroom has just started the race

FINISH Suzie Celery has just finished the race

INSIDE Emma Apple is having tea inside the house

OUTSIDE Pippa Pear is outside the house

OVER Supercool is jumping over the hurdle

UNDER Olive is sitting under the hurdle

MORE OPPOSITES

Hard Soft

Light Dark

Stand Sit

Good Bad

Rough Smooth

Mommy Daddy

Young Old

Shallow Deep

Rich Poor

Day Night

Up Down

Girl Boy

Odd Even

Quiet Noisy

After Before

Silly Sensible